A STUDY IN
STATEMENTS

A STUDY IN STATEMENTS

The pocket-sized guide to financial statements

HOLLY ZHANG

ISBN: 978-1-0688034-1-3

For mom

TABLE OF CONTENTS

FOREWORD

In *A Study in Statements*, Holly aims to demystify the world of financial statements and related accounting practices. Drawing from her exceptional aptitude in my accounting class, Holly has crafted a comprehensive resource that caters to both novice learners and seasoned professionals alike. Through clear explanations and practical examples, readers will gain an understanding of the three financial statements.

Holly's book empowers readers with the knowledge to make informed decisions in their personal and professional lives. Whether you're an aspiring entrepreneur or simply someone seeking to enhance their financial literacy, *A Study in Statements* offers invaluable insights that go beyond simply crunching numbers. With Holly's dedication to excellence and her passion in the subject matter, this book serves as a testament to her commitment to providing others with the tools they need to navigate the realm of financial literacy with confidence and proficiency.

- Ms. Lai, *Accounting 11 Teacher*

LETTER TO READER

I hope you enjoy this book as much as I enjoyed writing it. As you read through each section, I hope you realize financial statements go beyond the semantic definitions of line items and accounting regulations; they tell the stories of a business. I write with the intention of clearing the smokescreen around finance and introducing concepts that are readily applicable to your life.

This book covers the fundamentals of financial statements. At the end of each section, there are exercises and lists of key terms to consolidate knowledge. All statements used in this book can be retrieved from the Securities Exchange Commission's Electronic, Data Gathering, Analysis, and Retrieval database. I wish you an informative read!

Sincerely,

Holly

SECTION 1.
ON FINANCIAL STATEMENTS

INTRODUCTION

 Understand the purpose and users of financial statements.

A financial statement is a record that reveals the business's financial position. The financial position of a business reflects the financial health. By reporting figures like assets, net income, and cash flow, financial statements provide insight into the business's potential and stability. Financial statements are used by internal users like the business's management and external users like investors, creditors, and suppliers.

Internal users Internal users are individuals within the business. An example of an internal user is the management team, who uses financial statements to make holistic business decisions. For instance, to determine which operations to invest in, executives may review the business's largest sources of revenue. Other uses include the management of the business's loans and other liabilities. Overall, financial statements help businesses make informed decisions.

External users   External users are individuals outside of the business who do not participate in its day-to-day activities. The business's investors are one of the largest groups of external users. They may use financial statements to evaluate the business's performance. Other examples of external users include creditors and suppliers, who may use the business's financial statements to assess how well it is at handling its liabilities. There are many types of external users who each have different look-fors in the business's financial statements, but ultimately, they read these statements to make informed decisions.

In many countries, publicly traded companies are legally obliged to prepare and submit financial statements to regulators. In the United States, the law obligates public companies to file relevant information with the Securities Exchange Commission (SEC). Companies do this through the SEC's Electronic Data Gathering, Analysis, and Retrieval (EDGAR) database, which contains all the financial records of publicly traded companies on American stock exchanges. The following is a list of the most commonly used forms submitted by companies to EDGAR.

Form 10-K The annual report of the company. It includes the company's business activities, financial statements, and future plans.

Form 10-Q Quarterly report of the company. It includes the company's financial statements, earnings, and financial performance for the quarter.

Form 8-K Current report. It discloses any material event that happens within the company (e.g. a change in management).

Proxy statemen Additional information about management including salaries and benefits.

KEY TERMS

Financial statement	A record of the business's financial position and activities
Financial position	The business's financial health
Internal user	Individuals belonging to the business (e.g. management)
External user	Individuals outside of the business (e.g. investors)
Securities Exchange Commission (SEC)	U.S. government securities regulator
Electronic Data Gathering, Analysis, and Retrieval	Database of public companies' financial records maintained by the SEC

EXERCISES

1. **What is a financial statement?**

   a. A record of a business's financial position
   b. An entry of a business's transactions
   c. A log of a business's activities
   d. A spreadsheet of a business's value

2. **Which of the following is NOT an external user?**

   a. Government
   b. Auditors
   c. Management
   d. Creditors

3. **Which of the following is NOT an internal user?**

   a. Suppliers
   b. Owners
   c. Managers
   d. CEO

4. **What is the main purpose of the SEC?**

   a. To regulate financial markets
   b. To set interest rates
   c. To conduct fiscal policy
   d. To protect consumers

Answers: 1. a; 2. c.; 3. a.; 4. a

TYPES OF FINANCIAL STATEMENTS

 Understand the definitions of the three financial statements.

There are three main financial statements: the balance sheet, income statement, and cash flow statement. This section gives a brief overview of them.

Balance sheet   The balance sheet is a snapshot of the business's assets, liabilities, and shareholders' equity. It is called a snapshot because there exists one at any given point in time. Assets are what the business owns. Liabilities are what the business owes to third parties like banks. Equity is what the business owes to its shareholders. The formula known as the accounting equation reflects the relationship between the three components of the balance sheet:

$$assets = liabilities + equity$$

It can be rearranged to:

$$equity = assets - liabilities$$

This presents equity as the business's net worth. Net worth is the value left after assets have been liquidated and liabilities have been paid.

Income statement The income statement is a statement of the business's profitability. Unlike a balance sheet, it does not exist at any given point in time; it is periodic. The income statement contains two components: revenue and expenses. When expanded, the income statement reveals specific types of income and expenses useful for more specific analysis. The income statement shows how the business's revenue is transformed into its net income.

Cash flow statement The cash flow statement illustrates the movement of cash entering and exiting the business. It is periodic and is broken down into three categories: Operating activities, investing activities, and financing activities. Operating activities are the day-to-day activities of the business. Examples include conducting sales, purchasing inventory, and paying wages. Investing activities are the purchases and sales of long-term physical assets and other investments. Examples include the purchase of equipment and sale of property. Financing activities are the activities that raise funds for the business. Examples include taking out loans and issuing shares.

KEY TERMS

Balance sheet	Snapshot of the business's assets, liabilities, equity
Income statement	Statement of the business's profitability
Cash flow statement	Statement of the business's cash movement

EXERCISES

1. **What is the accounting equation?**

    a. Assets = liabilities + equity
    b. Assets = liabilities - equity
    c. Assets = liabilities
    d. Assets = equity

2. **On which statement can you find a business's assets?**

    a. Balance sheet
    b. Income statement
    c. Cash flow statement
    d. Statement of retained earnings

3. **Which statement calculates net income?**

    a. Balance sheet
    b. Income statement
    c. Cash flow statement
    d. Statement of changes in equity

4. **What is the purpose of a cash flow statement?**

    a. To report net income
    b. To show changes in equity
    c. To illustrate cash movement

d. To reveal the business's worth

5. **Which statement is a snapshot of a business's financial position?**

   a. Balance sheet
   b. Income statement
   c. Cash flow statement
   d. Statement of retained earnings

6. **Where would you find information about a business's liabilities?**

   a. Balance sheet
   b. Income statement
   c. Cash flow statement
   d. Statement of changes in equity

Answers: 1. a.; 2. a.; 3. b.; 4. c.; 5. a.; 6. a.

GENERALLY ACCEPTED ACCOUNTING PRINCIPLES

 Understand the purpose of GAAP and its two cornerstone principles.

The Generally Accepted Accounting Principles (GAAP) are a set of accounting standards that dictate how to prepare and present financial statements. They are the rules we follow in financial reporting. GAAP ensures consistency and transparency across different industries. It follows a method of accounting known as accrual-based accounting. In accrual-based accounting, revenue is recognized when it is earned and expenses when they are incurred. To understand the definition of accrual-based accounting, consider this example:

A large business contracted a cleaning service for one of its facilities on December 20th. The total bill is $5000 and the business has one month to pay. When recording its expenses for the calendar year (January to December), does the business include this cleaning service expense? Or does the business include it for the next year when the payment is due?

According to accrual-based accounting, the business should record this expense for the current year. Although it is true the business does not have to pay for the cleaning service in December, it did receive the service in that month. As a result, the business must recognize this transaction in December. This is what it means to recognize expenses when they are incurred. If the business does not recognize this expense in December, it can misrepresent its expenses for that specific period. The same concept applies for revenue. Consider the same example from the perspective of the cleaning service:

Although the cleaning service was contracted in December, it will receive payment from its client in one month. However, according to accrual-based accounting, it still records its revenue in December, even though no cash was received. This is because the cleaning—the action that earned the revenue—was performed in December. This is why we say revenue is recognized when it is earned and not when it is received.

Accrual-based accounting is illustrated in two of GAAP's most important principles: revenue recognition and matching principle.

Revenue recognition   Revenue recognition states that we recognize revenue when it is earned, not when cash is received. The actual payment of cash does not affect when revenue is recognized. Delivery of the good or execution of the service allows for revenue recognition.

Matching principle   The matching principle states that expenses must be recorded in the same period in which they made efforts to generate revenue. Consider a business that sells pens. Let's say the business has 2000 pens in stock, each of which costs $5 to produce, and sold half its inventory (1000). According to the Matching Principle, it must recognize 1000 of those pens as a cost of sale. The business does not recognize all 2000 pens—in other words, its inventory—as an expense as only half of those pens were sold to generate revenue.

KEY TERMS

Accrual-based accounting

Method of accounting in which revenue is recognized when it is earned and expenses when incurred

Generally Accepted Accounting Principles

Set of accounting regulations

Revenue Recognition

Accounting principle that states revenue is recognized when it is earned, not when cash is received

Matching Principle

Accounting principle that states expenses must be recorded in the same period in which they made efforts to generate revenue

EXERCISES

1. **Revenue is recognized when...**

   a. Cash is received
   b. Service is performed
   c. Expenses are paid
   d. Expenses are incurred

2. **Expenses are recognized when...**

   a. They are incurred
   b. They are paid
   c. Revenue is recognized
   d. Bill is received

3. **A streaming service has a monthly subscription for customers to access content. When does the service recognize revenue?**

4. **What is the point of the matching principle?**

   a. To recognize revenue when earned
   b. To match expenses with the revenue generated
   c. To delay expense recognition
   d. To accelerate expense recognition

Answers: 1. b.; 2. a.; 3. Answers may vary. Example: Over time as the customer uses the service; 4. b.

SECTION 2.
ON BALANCE SHEETS

ACCOUNTING EQUATION

 Understand the accounting equation and its components.

The balance sheet is a snapshot of the business's assets, liabilities, and equity. The relationship between these three components is illustrated through the accounting equation:

$$assets = liabilities + equity$$

The accounting equation states that the things the business owns must equal the things the business owes. Assets are what the business owns. Liabilities are what the business owes to third parties like banks. Equity is what the business owes to shareholders. Another way of viewing the balance sheet is a record of the business's worth. When rearranged, the accounting equation becomes:

$$equity = assets - liabilities$$

This presents equity as the net worth of the business, calculated by the value left over after assets are converted into cash and liabilities are paid off.

KEY TERMS

Balance sheet	Snapshot of the business's assets, liabilities, and equity
Accounting equation	assets = liabilities + equity
Assets	What the business owns
Liabilities	What the business owes to third parties
Equity	What the business owes to shareholders (net worth)

EXERCISES

1. **Assets**: $10,000; **liabilities**: $50,000. Calculate the **equity**.

2. **Assets**: $100,000; **liabilities**: $60,000. Calculate the **equity**.

3. **Liabilities**: $20,000; **equity**: $45,000. Calculate the **assets**.

4. **Liabilities**: $40,000; **equity**: $15,000. Calculate the **assets**.

5. **Assets**: $100,000; **equity**: $50,000. Calculate the **liabilities**.

6. **Assets**: $70,000; **equity**: $25,000. Calculate the **liabilities**.

Answers: 1. $(60,000); 2. $40,000; 3. $65,000; 4. $55,000; 5. $150,000; 6. $45,000.

ASSETS

 Understand the definition of an asset and the types of assets on the balance sheet.

The assets of the business are what the business owns. On the balance sheet, they are grouped into two categories: current and noncurrent. Current assets are considered liquid, or easily convertible into cash. They include cash, accounts receivable (A/R), and inventory. These accounts are expected to be used up within twelve months. Noncurrent assets, on the other hand, are long-term. Tangible, noncurrent assets include property, plant, and equipment (PP&E). Intangible, noncurrent assets include intellectual property and goodwill. On the balance sheet, assets are listed in order of liquidity from most liquid to least.

Below is the asset section of Apple's Q3 balance sheet from June 29, 2024 (in millions)[i].

Current assets:

Cash and cash equivalents	25,565
Marketable securities	36,236
Accounts receivable, net	22,795
Vendor non-trade receivables	20,377
Inventories	6,165
Other current assets	14,297
Total current assets	125,435

Noncurrent assets:

Marketable securities	91,240
PPE, net	44,502
Other non-current assets	70,435
Total noncurrent assets	206,177
Total assets	331,612

Marketable securities   Marketable securities are financial securities like stocks and bonds owned by the business. Depending on the expiry date of the securities, they may be classified as current or noncurrent. Apple had around $127 billion in current and noncurrent marketable securities for the quarter.

A/R   A/R is money due to the business from the sale of goods or services. It can be considered as a line of credit extended over a short-term period. Non-trade receivables are another type on receivables unrelated to the business's normal operations. Apple had around $22.7 billion in A/R.

Inventory   Inventory contains the goods the business intends to sell, work-in-progress products, and raw materials. For example, if a bakery's final good is bread, then the work-in-progress might be the dough, and the raw materials might be flour and sugar. Apple had around $6 billion in inventory.

PP&E   These are long term (noncurrent) assets that are expected to last longer than a year. They include buildings, equipment, and land. Apple had around $44.5 billion in PP&E.

Intellectual property   Intellectual property does not appear on the balance sheet but is still considered an asset. It includes the business's trademarks, copyrights, and patents on specific good or services.

Goodwill   In acquisitions, this is the premium, or additional, amount paid for the business. It is the difference between the business's purchase value and book value (equity). Factors contributing to goodwill include brand and reputation.

KEY TERMS

Current asset	Asset expected to be used up within a year
A/R	Money due to the business from sale of goods or services
Inventory	The goods the business intends to sell, work-in progress products and raw materials
Noncurrent asset	Asset expected to last longer than a year
PP&E	Property, plant, and equipment
Intellectual property	Trademarks, copyrights, patents
Goodwill	Premium amount paid for the business during takeovers
Tangible asset	Physical asset
Intangible asset	Non-physical asset
Liquidity	The ability to convert something into cash

EXERCISES

1. **Which of the following is considered a current asset?**

    a. Office building
    b. Inventory
    c. Patents
    d. Truck

2. **Which of the following is NOT considered a current asset?**

    a. Cash
    b. Accounts receivable
    c. Marketable securities
    d. Goodwill

3. **Which of the following is classified as a noncurrent asset?**

    a. Supplies
    b. Inventory
    c. Marketable securities
    d. Land

4. **What distinguishes current assets from noncurrent assets?**

    a. Tangibility

    b. Liquidity

    c. Time

    d. Depreciation

5. **Which of the following is NOT considered a marketable security?**

    a. Bonds

    b. Stocks

    c. Real estate

    d. Mutual funds

Answers: 1. b.; 2. d.; 3. d. 4. b.; 5. c

LIABILITIES

 Understand the definition of a liability and the types of liabilities on the balance sheet.

Liabilities are what the business owes to third parties. Just like assets, liabilities are grouped into current and noncurrent. Current liabilities are expected to be paid or matured within twelve months. They include things like accounts payable (A/P), deferred revenue, and accrued expenses. Noncurrent liabilities are longer term, including loans, lease liabilities, and notes payable.

Below is the liability section of Apple's Q3 balance sheet from June 29, 2024 (in millions)[ii].

Current liabilities:	
Accounts payable	47,574
Other current liabilities	60,889
Deferred revenue	8,053
Commercial paper	2,994
Term debt	12,114
Total current liabilities	131,624

Noncurrent assets:	125,435
Term debt	86,196
Other noncurrent liabilities	47,084
Total noncurrent liabilities	133,280
Total liabilities	264,904

A/P A/P is money owed to creditors, suppliers, vendors, etc. It is a short-term debt obligation. Apple owed around $47.8 billion in A/P for the quarter.

Deferred revenue Deferred (unearned) revenue is money received in advance for a good or service. It is considered a liability because companies must provide their good or service to earn the revenue. Apple had around $8 billion in deferred revenue. This makes sense as Apple offers many software subscriptions and financing programs.

Commercial paper Commercial paper is a short-term debt obligation usually used to finance things like A/P and payroll. Apple owed around $2 billion in commercial paper.

Term debt Term debt can be current or noncurrent depending on the contract between the lender and borrower. Apple owed around $12 billion in term debt.

Accrued expenses Although not explicitly on Apple's balance sheet, accrued expenses is a common line item. They are expenses that have been incurred, but have not been paid for. For example, salaries may be paid the week after the period in which they occurred, so the business may accrue salary expenses during that time frame.

Lease liability Although not explicitly on Apple's balance sheet, lease liability is a common line item. It is the value of outstanding lease payments. Leases are long-term contracts in which a leaser rents an asset like equipment to a lessee.

Notes payable Notes payables are long-term debt obligations. They may represent the outstanding amount of a loan.

KEY TERMS

Current liability	Liability expected to mature (be paid off) within twelve months
A/P	Money owed to creditors, suppliers, vendors, etc.
Commercial paper	Short-term debt obligation used to finance things like A/P or payroll
Deferred revenue	Money received in advance for a good or service
Accrued expenses	Expenses that have been incurred, but not yet paid for in cash
Noncurrent liability	Liability expected to mature after a year
Lease liability	Value of outstanding lease payments
Notes payable	Long-term debt obligations

EXERCISES

1. **Which of the following is considered a current liability?**

   a. Accounts payable
   b. Commercial paper
   c. Unearned revenue
   d. All of the above

2. **Which of the following can be considered a noncurrent liability?**

   a. Term debt
   b. Accounts payable
   c. Notes payable (due within six months)
   d. Deferred revenue

3. **What is true about current liabilities?**

   a. They include debt due beyond one year
   b. They must be settled within one year
   c. They are tangible liabilities
   d. They mature within two years

Answers: 1. d.; 2. a.; 3. b.

SHAREHOLDERS' EQUITY

 Understand the definition of equity and equity on the balance sheet.

Shareholders' equity is the net worth of the business. It is the value of the business after its assets have been liquidated and debts have been paid. It is also the money owed by the business to its shareholders. The shareholders' equity section contains the business's share capital (stock) and retained earnings (accumulated profit/deficit).

Below is the abridged shareholders' equity section of Apple's Q3 balance sheet from June 29, 2024 (in millions)[iii]. Note: accum. = accumulated

Shareholders' equity:

Stock & add'l paid-in capital	79,850
Accumulated deficit	(4,726)
Accum. other comprehensive loss	(8,416)
Total shareholders' equity	66,708

Share capital Share capital is the money raised by issuing shares. Shares represent a fraction of the company. Common shares can be traded on exchanges. They give voting rights for the company's board of directors. There are also preferred shares, which do not give voting rights, but priority in returns. **Additional paid-in capital** is the additional amount paid for the stock during its initial public offering (IPO). Apple had almost $80 billion in common stock and additional paid-in capital for the quarter. It does not issue preferred shares.

Retained earnings Retained earnings are the cumulative profit of the business after dividend payments, if any. Some businesses will call it accumulated profit or deficit (e.g. Apple). Apple had a deficit of around $4.7 billion in retained earnings.

previous period's RE + net income – dividends

KEY TERMS

Shareholders' equity	Amount remaining after assets are liquidated and liabilities are paid
Share capital	Money raised by issuing shares
Additional paid-in capital	Additional amount for the stock during its IPO
Retained earnings	Previous period's retained earnings plus net income less dividends

EXERCISES

---

1. **Which of the following is NOT part of equity?**

    a. Receivables
    b. Share capital
    c. Retained earnings
    d. Stock

2. **Which of the following is NOT part of retained earnings?**

    a. Dividends
    b. Revenue
    c. Expenses
    d. Cash

3. **Which of the following best describes equity?**

    a. Business's earnings
    b. Business's net worth
    c. Business's debt
    d. Business's premium

4. **What is NOT a feature of common stock?**

    a. Voting rights
    b. Priority in dividend payouts

c. Ownership
d. Growth potential

5. **Revenue**: $100,000; **expenses**: $30,000; **dividends**: $10,000; **previous retained earnings**: $350,000. Calculate **retained earnings**.

6. **Revenue**: $300,000; **expenses**: $170,000; **dividends**: none; **previous retained earnings**: $120,000. Calculate **retained earnings**.

Answers: 1. a.; 2. d.; 3. b.; 4. b.; 5. $410,000; 6. $250,000.

PUTTING IT TOGETHER

 Understand how to read a complete balance sheet.

Below is Apple's Q3 balance sheet from 2024[iv].

ASSETS:

Current assets:

Cash and cash equivalents	25,565
Marketable securities	36,236
Accounts receivable, net	22,795
Vendor non-trade receivables	20,377
Inventories	6,165
Other current assets	14,297
Total current assets	125,435

Noncurrent assets:

Marketable securities	91,240
PPE, net	44,502
Other non-current assets	70,435
Total noncurrent assets	206,177
Total assets	331,612

LIABILITIES AND SHAREHOLDERS' EQUITY:

Current liabilities:	
Accounts payable	47,574
Other current liabilities	60,889
Deferred revenue	8,053
Commercial paper	2,994
Term debt	12,114
Total current liabilities	131,624
Noncurrent liabilities:	
Term debt	86,196
Other noncurrent liabilities	47,084
Total noncurrent liabilities	133,280
Total liabilities	264,904
Shareholders' equity	
Common stock & additional paid-in capital	79,850
Accumulated deficit (retained earnings)	(4,726)
Accumulated other comprehensive loss	(8,416)
Total shareholders' equity	66,708
Total liabilities & equity	331,612

SECTION 3.
ON INCOME STATEMENTS

REVENUE AND EXPENSES

 Understand revenue and the types of expenses on the income statement.

The income statement presents the business's profitability. It is comprised of two components: revenue and expenses. When expanded, the income statement shows the revenue's transformation into its net income. Below is the Q3 income statement of Apple in 2024 (in millions)[v]. In this section, we will discuss its revenue and expenses. In **Section 3.2**, we will discuss how to calculate types of income.

Net sales:	
Product	61,564
Services	24,213
Total net sales	85,777
Cost of sales:	
Products	39,803
Services	6,296
Total cost of sales	46,099
Gross margin	39,678

Operating expenses:

Research and development	8,006
Selling, general, and administrative	6,320
Total operating expenses	14,326
Operating income	25,352
Other income/(expense), net	142
Income before provision for income taxes	25,494
Provision for income taxes	4,046
Net income	21,448

Revenue Revenue is the money generated from the business's operations. It comes from the sale of goods and/or services. It is considered the top line of the business. Apple made around $85 billion in revenue for the quarter.

Cost of sales The cost of sales, or cost of goods sold, is the direct expenses incurred to produce a good or service. Direct expenses may come from labour and raw materials. They depend on the number of goods or services sold. For example, a bakery's cost of sales may include flour and the bakers' wages. Apple had around $46 billion in cost of sales.

Operating expenses   Operating expenses are indirect, overhead expenses incurred during the day-to-day activities of the business. Common types of operating expenses include marketing, research and development, depreciation, and selling, general, and administrative (SG&A) expenses. Apple had around $14.3 billion in operating expenses.

Research and development (R&D)   R&D represents the costs incurred to improve the goods or services of the business. Unlike most operating expenses, R&D is not expected to immediately generate profit and instead is expected to benefit the business in the long-term. Apple had around $8 billion in R&D.

Depreciation   Depreciation reflects the value lost from an asset over time. Note that is it a non-cash expense, meaning no cash is spent to reflect depreciation. For example, a truck may depreciate $5000 in value annually to reflect its usage.

Selling, general, and administrative (SG&A)   These represent the overhead costs of the business including the salaries, utilities, and rent.

SG&A also includes selling and marketing expenses. Apple had around $6.3 billion in SG&A.

Non-operating expenses Interest and income taxes are common non-operating expenses. Interest is the charge on borrowing money. Interest rates are outside of the business's control, which is why interest is not as important as something like operating expenses when analyzing income statements. Because tax rates are also outside of the business's control, they are not as important as other expenses when analyzing profitability. Some companies may pay more in taxes and others may pay less depending on their area's tax laws. Apple had around $4 billion in taxes.

KEY TERMS

Income statement	Statement of the business's profitability
Net revenue (sales)	Revenue minus discounts and returns
Cost of sales	Direct costs incurred to provide a good or service
Operating expenses	Expenses incurred by the business's day-to-day operations
Non-operating expenses	Expenses that do not directly contribute to the business's operations

EXERCISES

1. **What is the top line of the income statement?**

   a. COGS
   b. Revenue
   c. Net income
   d. Interest expense

2. **Which of the following is considered a COGS?**

   a. Utilities
   b. Marketing
   c. Raw materials
   d. Depreciation on equipment

3. **Which of the following is NOT considered an operating expense?**

   a. Rent
   b. Depreciation
   c. Interest
   d. Research and development

4. **Which of the following is considered a non-cash expense?**

   a. Interest
   b. Depreciation

c. Marketing

d. Utilities

5. **What is the bottom line of the income statement?**

a. Revenue

b. Operating expenses

c. Net income

d. Gross income

Answers: 1. b.; 2. c.; 3. c.; 4. b.; 5. c.

INCOME TYPES

 Understand the types of income and their purpose on the income statement.

While the business's net income is important, it is not everything; analysts will also look at other metrics of income on the income statement to assess the business's profitability. Below is Apple's Q3 income statement from 2024 (in millions)[vi].

Net sales:	
Product	61,564
Services	24,213
Total net sales	85,777
Cost of sales:	
Products	39,803
Services	6,296
Total cost of sales	46,099
Gross margin	39,678
Operating expenses:	
Research and development	8,006
Selling, general, and administrative	6,320

Total operating expenses	14,326
Operating income	25,352
Other income/(expense), net	142
Income before provision for income taxes	25,494
Provision for income taxes	4,046
Net income	21,448

Gross income Gross income, sometimes called gross margin, is the money remaining after deducting the cost of sales from revenue. It is a better indicator of profitability when specifically measuring the good or service's performance. Apple made almost $40 billion in gross income for the quarter.

Operating income Operating income is the money remaining after deducting operating expenses from gross income. It measures the measure's operational performance and shows analysts how well the business is at managing costs related to its day-to-day operations. Apple made around $25 billion in operating income.

Income before taxes Income before taxes is the money remaining after deducting non-operating expenses (e.g. interest) from operating income. Because tax rates are not determined by the business, tax expenses can vary significantly within industries. As a result, when gauging performance and comparing the business against others, analysts may prefer income before taxes to net income. Income before taxes more accurately reflects the business's control over its expense and revenue. Apple made around $25 billion in income before taxes.

Net income   Net income is the bottom line of the business. It is the money remaining after all expenses relevant to the business have been deducted from revenue. Net income is helpful in learning about the overall profitability and cost control of the business. Apple made around $21.4 billion in net income.

In addition to these income types, there are also other metrics that analysts use. Common metrics are earnings before interest and tax (EBIT) and earnings before interest, tax, and depreciation (ETBIDA).

EBIT   EBIT ignores interest and tax in its calculation of profitability. Interest rates, like tax rates, fall outside of the business's control. By ignoring interest and tax, analysts can better gauge the direct impact of operations on the business.

EBITDA   EBITDA takes EBIT a step further by further excluding depreciation and amortization (i.e. depreciation of intangible assets) its calculation of income. Depreciation and amortization are non-cash expenses, so by excluding them, EBITDA provides a clearer picture of the business's operational cash flow. In **Section 4.2**, we will further discuss operational cash flow.

KEY TERMS

Gross income	Revenue less cost of sales
Operating income	Gross income less operating expenses
Income before taxes	Operating income less non-operating expenses
Net income	Revenue less total expenses
EBIT	Earnings before interest and tax
EBITDA	Earnings before interest, tax, depreciation, and amortization

EXERCISES

1. **How is gross income (margin) calculated?**

    a. Revenue less operating expenses
    b. Revenue less interest and tax expenses
    c. Revenue less depreciation expense
    d. Revenue less COGS

2. **What is NOT included in calculating operating income?**

    a. Product revenue
    b. Service revenue
    c. Interest income
    d. Gross income

3. **Revenue**: $250,000; **COGS**: $100,000. Calculate **gross income.**

4. **Revenue**: $300,000; **COGS**: $200,000; **operating expenses**: $150,000. Calculate **operating income.**

5. **Revenue**: $180,000; **COGS**: $120,000; **operating expenses**: $60,000; **interest**: $20,000. Calculate **net income.**

6.   **Net income**: $600,000; **tax**: $100,000; **interest**: $150,000. Calculate **income before tax.**

7.   **Revenue**: $100,000; **COGS**: $25,000; **depreciation**: $1000; **operating expenses (excl. depreciation)**: $10,000; **interest**: $1,500; **tax**: $6250. Calculate **EBITDA.**

8.   **Net income**: $500,000; **tax**: $100,000; **interest**: $50,000; **depreciation**: $75,000; **amortization**: $25,000. Calculate **ETBIDA.**

Answers: 1. d.; 2. c.; 3. $150,000; 4. $(50,000); 5. $(20,000); 6. $850,000; 7. $65,000; 8. $750,000.

PUTTING IT TOGETHER

 Understand the income statement with all sections expanded.

Below is Apple's Q3 income statement from 2024[vii]. Notice how the revenue is broken down into various profits and transformed into the bottom line.

Net sales:

Product	61,564
Services	24,213
Total net sales	85,777

Cost of sales:

Products	39,803
Services	6,296
Total cost of sales	46,099
Gross margin	39,678

Operating expenses:

Research and development	8,006
Selling, general, and administrative	6,320

Total operating expenses	14,326
Operating income	25,352
Other income/(expense), net	142
Income before provision for income taxes	25,494
Provision for income taxes	4,046
Net income	21,448

SECTION 4.

ON CASH FLOW STATEMENTS

CASH FLOW

Understand cash flow and its importance to businesses.

The cash flow statement illustrates the movement of cash into and out of the business. A positive cash flow is important because it allows businesses to pay debts, reinvest into the business, return money to shareholders, and expand operations. More often than not, businesses file bankruptcies because of poor cash flow management. While the balance sheet and income statement follow accrual-based accounting, the cash flow statement follows cash-based accounting.

The cash flow statement has three components: operating activities, investing activities, and financing activities. It calculates the cash flows of each activity to arrive at the ending balance of cash. Below is an example of a cash flow statement. It opens with the beginning cash balance (i.e. cash held from previous years) and is adjusted with operating, investing, and financing cash flows to arrive at the ending cash balance.

Cash and cash equivalents, beginning balances
Operating activities
      Cash generated by operating activities
Investing activities
      Cash generated by investing activities
Financing activities
      Cash generated financing activities
Cash, cash equivalents, ending balances

KEY TERMS

Cash flow statement	Statement of the business's cash movement
Operating activities	Day-to-day activities of the business
Investing activities	Purchases and sales of noncurrent, tangible assets and other investments
Financing activities	Activities that raise and return capital to investors

EXERCISES

1. **Which section of the cash flow statement includes cash movement of business operations?**

    a. Operating activities
    b. Investing activities
    c. Financing activities
    d. Capital activities

2. **Which of the following is considered an investing activity?**

    a. Cash paid to suppliers
    b. Cash paid for interest expenses
    c. Cash received from issuing stock
    d. Cash paid to purchase PP&E

3. **Which of the following is NOT considered a financing activity?**

    a. Cash dividends paid to shareholders
    b. Cash received from bank loan
    c. Cash paid to purchase inventory
    d. Cash received from issuing bonds

4. **What can a positive cash flow indicate?**

    a. The business is losing money

b. The business has enough cash to sustain operations
c. The business has ineffective cost control
d. The business has a cash outflow

Answers: 1. a.; 2. d.; 3. c. 4. b.

OPERATING ACTIVITIES

 Understand cash flow and its importance to businesses.

Operating activities are the day-to-day activities of the business that allow it to generate revenue. Below are the operating activities of Apple's Q3 cash flow statement (in millions)[viii].

Net income	79,000
Adjustments	
Depreciation and amortization	8,534
Share-based compensation	8,830
Other	(1,964)
Changes in operating assets and liabilities	
Accounts receivable, net	6,697
Vendor non-trade receivables	11,100
Inventories	41
Other current & NC assets	(5,626)
Accounts payable	(15,171)
Other current & noncurrent liabilities	2
Cash generated by operating activities	91,443

Net income The operating activities section opens with net income, making adjustments to reflect cash-only transactions. These adjustments reconcile net income to cash from operating activities.

Adjustments to net income Operating activities include adjustments to net income to reflect the business's cash flow. For example, depreciation and amortization are non-cash expenses, so they are added back to net income. Apple had around $8.5 billion in depreciation and amortization expenses for the quarter. Share-based compensation is a non-cash expense as it is paid in shares, so it is also added back to net income.

Changes in operating assets and liabilities Changes in operating assets and liabilities refer to the change across periods. Change in receivables, for example, is the difference between last year's receivables ending balance and this year's receivables ending balance.

Receivables Positive receivables (i.e. cash outflow) on the cash flow statement indicate fewer receivables outstanding this year compared to the last. This means the business collected more cash from sales this year. As a result, on Apple has cash inflow of around $6.6 billion in A/R payments.

Inventory   Positive inventory (i.e. cash inflow) indicates less inventory on hand this year. This implies a higher turnover as more of the inventory was sold. Apple has cash inflow of around $41 million from inventory.

Payables   Negative payables indicate the business made more cash payments this year than it did in the previous. This represents money leaving the business, so it is a cash outflow. Apple has a cash outflow of around $15 billion in A/P payments.

KEY TERMS

Operating cash flow   Cash from the business's operating activities

Operating activities   Day-to-day activities of the business

EXERCISES

---

1. **Which of the following is considered a cash inflow from operating activities?**

    a. Cash received from selling equipment
    b. Cash received from customers for sales
    c. Cash paid for purchasing property
    d. Cash paid for debt repayment

2. **Which of the following is NOT included in the calculation for cash from operating activities?**

    a. Depreciation expense
    b. Cash payments to suppliers
    c. Accounts receivable
    d. Cash paid for dividends

3. **How is the change in A/R treated in the operating activities section?**

    a. Increase in A/R is added to net income
    b. Decrease in A/R is added to net income
    c. Increase in A/R is subtracted from net income
    d. Decrease in A/R is subtracted from net income

Answers: 1. b.; 2. d.; 3. c.

INVESTING ACTIVITIES

 Understand cash from investing activities and the components of it.

Investing activities are the purchases and sales of noncurrent, tangible assets and other investments. Examples of investing activities include the purchase of PP&E and sale of securities like stocks. Below are the investing activities of Apple's Q3 cash flow statement (in millions)[ix]. Note: mark. sec. = marketable securities

Purchases of marketable securities	(38,074)
Proceeds from maturities of mark. sec.	39,838
Proceeds from sales of mark. sec.	7,382
Payments for acquisition of PP&E	(6,539)
Other	(1,117)
Cash generated by investing activities	1,490

Marketable securities Marketable securities are financial assets like stocks and bonds that can be sold and purchased. They can be cash outflows or inflows depending on what the business chooses to do with them (i.e. purchase or sell).

Property, plant, and equipment P&E are noncurrent, tangible assets. The purchase (or sale) of them is considered an investment activity. Other examples of investing activities related to PP&E are capital expenditures, the money used by business to purchase, maintain, or expand PP&E. Apple has around a cash outflow of around $6.5 billion from payments for PP&E for the quarter.

KEY TERMS

Investing cash flow	Cash from the business's investing activities
Investing activities	Purchases and sales of noncurrent, tangible assets and other investments
Capital expenditures	Money used to buy, expand, or maintain long-term, physical assets

EXERCISES

1. **Which of the following is considered an investing activity?**

    a. Cash received from interest income
    b. Cash paid for purchasing equipment
    c. Cash paid for debt repayment
    d. Cash paid for interest expense

2. **How do the sales of noncurrent, physical assets affect the investing activities' cash flow?**

    a. Cash outflow
    b. Cash inflow
    c. No effect
    d. Sales of noncurrent, physical assets are recorded under financing activities

3. **Which of the following is NOT considered a capital expenditure?**

    a. Sale of property
    b. Sale of equipment
    c. Purchase of marketable securities
    d. Purchase of truck

Answers: 1. b.; 2. b.; 3. c

FINANCING ACTIVITIES

 Understand cash from investing activities and the components of it.

Financing activities are the activities that raise and return capital to investors. Examples of financing activities include the repayment of debt, issuance of stock, and payment of dividends. Below are the abridged financing activities of Apple's Q3 cash flow statement (in millions)[x].

Payment for taxes	(5,163)
Payments for dividends and equivalents	(11,430)
Repurchases of common stock	(69,866)
Repayments of term debt	(7,400)
Repayments of commercial paper, net	(2,985)
Other	(191)
Cash used in financing activities	(97,035)

Payments   Payments for taxes, dividends, debt, and other obligations are cash outflows. It is normal for the business to have a lot of cash outflow in the financing activities section as they are returning capital to investors and paying debt.

Repurchases of common stock
Businesses may repurchase their own stock to increase the value of the outstanding shares. Apple is known as one of the biggest repurchasers of its common stock. In its third quarter, Apple repurchased almost $70 billion in common stock. In May 2024, it announced a buyback of $110 billion[xi].

KEY TERMS

Financing cash flow	Cash from the business's financing activities
Financing activities	Activities that raise and return capital to investors

EXERCISES

---

1. **Which of the following is considered a cash inflow from financing activities?**

    a. Cash received from issuing new bonds
    b. Cash received from selling stocks
    c. Cash received from borrowing loan
    d. All of the above

2. **How do payments of dividends affect the financing activities' cash flow?**

    a. Cash outflow
    b. Cash inflow
    c. No effect
    d. Payment of dividends are recorded under investing activities

3. **How does repurchase of common stock affect the financing activities' cash flow?**

    a. Cash outflow
    b. Cash inflow
    c. No effect
    d. Repurchase of common stock is not possible

Answers: 1. d.; 2. a.; 3. a.

PUTTING IT TOGETHER

 Understand the cash flow statement with all three sections compiled.

Below is Apple's Q3 cash flow statement from 2024[xii]. It adjusts cash with cash flows from operating, investing, and financing activities to arrive at the ending balance. Note: NC = noncurrent; mark. sec. = marketable securities

Cash, cash equivalents, beginning balance	30,737
Operating activities:	
Net income	79,000
Adjustments	
Depreciation and amortization	8,534
Share-based compensation exp.	8,830
Other	(1,964)
Changes in operating assets and liabilities	

Accounts receivable, net	6,697
Vendor non-trade receivables	11,100
Inventories	41
Other current & NC assets	(5,626)
Accounts payable	(15,171)
Other current & NC liabilities	2
Cash from operating activities	(91,443)
Investing activities:	
Purchases of marketable securities	(38,074)
Proceeds from maturities of mark. sec.	39,838
Proceeds from sales of mark. sec.	7,382
Payments for acquisition of PP&E	(6,539)
Other	(1,117)
Cash from investing activities	1,490

Financing activities

Payments for taxes	(5,163)
Payments for dividends and equivalents	(11,430)
Repurchases of common stock	(69,866)
Repayments of term debt	(7,400)
Repayments of commercial paper, net	(2,985)
Other	(191)
Cash used in fin. Activities	(97,035)
Increase/(Decrease) in cash	(4,102)
Cash, cash equivalents, ending balance	26,635

INDEX

INTRODUCTION

KEY TERMS

Financial statement	Record of the business's financial position and activities
Financial position	The condition of the business's financial health
Internal user	Individuals belonging to the business (e.g. management)
External user	Individuals not belonging to the business
Securities Exchange Commission (SEC)	U.S. government securities regulator
Electronic Data Gathering, Analysis, and Retrieval (EDGAR)	Database of public companies' financial records maintained by the SEC.

TYPES OF FINANCIAL STATEMENTS

KEY TERMS

Balance sheet	Snapshot of the business's assets, liabilities, equity
Income statement	Statement of the business's profitability
Cash flow statement	Statement of the business's cash movement

GENERALLY ACCEPTED ACCOUNTING PRINCIPLES

KEY TERMS

Accrual-based accounting	Revenue is recognized when it is earned and expenses when incurred
Generally Accepted Accounting Principles	Set of accounting regulations
Revenue Recognition	Revenue is recognized when it is earned, not when cash is received
Performance obligation	The delivery of a good or execution of a service that the business is obligated to perform
Matching Principle	Expenses must be recorded in the same period in which they made efforts to generate revenue

ACCOUNTING EQUATION

KEY TERMS

Balance sheet	Snapshot of the business's assets, liabilities, and equity
Accounting equation	assets = liabilities plus equity
Assets	What the business owns
Liabilities	What the business owes to third parties
Equity	What the business owes to its shareholders (net worth)

ASSETS

KEY TERMS

Current asset	Asset expected to be used up within a year
A/R	Money due to the business from sale of goods or services
Inventory	The goods the business intends to sell, work-in progress products and
Noncurrent asset	Asset expected to last longer than a year
PP&E	Property, plant, and equipment
Intellectual property	Trademarks, copyrights, patents

Goodwill	Premium amount paid for the business during takeovers
Tangible asset	Physical asset
Intangible asset	Non-physical asset
Liquidity	The ability to convert something into cash

LIABILITIES

KEY TERMS

Current liability	Liability expected to mature (be paid off) within a year
A/P	Money owed to creditors, suppliers, vendors, etc.
Commercial paper	Short-term debt obligation used to finance things like A/P or payroll
Deferred revenue	Money received in advance for a good or service
Accrued expenses	Expenses that have been incurred, but not yet paid for in cash

Noncurrent liability	Liability expected to mature after a year
Lease liability	Value of outstanding lease payments
Notes payable	Long-term debt obligations

SHAREHOLDERS' EQUITY

KEY TERMS

Shareholders' equity	Amount remaining after assets are liquidated and liabilities are paid
Share capital	Money raised by issuing shares
Additional paid-in capital	Additional amount for the stock during its IPO
Retained earnings	Previous period's retained earnings plus net income less dividends

REVENUE AND EXPENSES

KEY TERMS

Income statement	Statement of the business's profitability
Net revenue (sales)	Revenue minus discounts and returns
Cost of sales	Direct costs incurred to provide a good or service
Operating expenses	Expenses incurred by the business's day-to-day operations
Non-operating expenses	Expenses that do not directly contribute to the business's operations

INCOME TYPES

KEY TERMS

Gross income	Revenue less cost of sales
Operating income	Gross income less operating expenses
Income before taxes	Operating income less non-operating expenses
Net income	Revenue less total expenses
EBIT	Earnings before interest and tax
EBITDA	Earnings before interest, tax, depreciation, and amortization

CASH FLOW

KEY TERMS

Cash flow statement	Statement of the business's cash movement
Operating activities	Day-to-day activities of the business
Investing activities	Purchases and sales of noncurrent, tangible assets and other investments
Financing activities	Activities that raise and return capital to investors

OPERATING ACTIVITIES

KEY TERMS

Operating cash flow	Cash from the business's operating activities
Operating activities	Day-to-day activities of the business

INVESTING ACTIVITIES

KEY TERMS

Investing cash flow

Cash from the business's investing activities

Investing activities

Purchases and sales of noncurrent, tangible assets and other investments

Capital expenditures

Money used to buy, expand, or maintain long-term, physical assets

FINANCING ACTIVITIES

KEY TERMS

Financing cash flow	Cash from the business's financing activities
Financing activities	Activities that raise and return capital to investors

BIBLIOGRAPHY

Apple Inc. 2024. *Form 10-Q.* Cupertino: Apple Inc.

Fernando, Jason. 2024. *Retained Earnings in Accounting and What They Can Tell You.* 25 June. Accessed December 28, 2024. https://www.investopedia.com/terms/r/retainedearnings.asp.

Hargrave, Marshall. 2024. *Goodwill (Accounting): What It Is, How It Works, and How To Calculate.* 28 June. Accessed December 27, 2023.

Kenton, Will. 2024. *Cash Flow From Investing Activities Explained: Types and Examples.* 01 August. Accessed March 24, 2024. https://www.investopedia.com/terms/c/cashflowfinvestingactivities.asp.

—. 2024. *What Is Gross Income? Definition, Formula, Calculation, and Example.* 24 May. Accessed January 18, 2024. https://www.investopedia.com/terms/g/grossincome.asp.

—. 2024. *What is Research and Development (R&D)?* 30 June. Accessed January 18, 2023. https://www.investopedia.com/terms/r/rardd.asp.

Liberto, Daniel. 2024. *Unearned Revenue: What It Is, How It Is Recorded and Reported.* 24 June. Accessed December 28, 2023. https://www.investopedia.com/terms/u/unearnedrevenue.asp.

Lin, BeiChen, and Ramis Najam. 2017. *Finance Simplified.*

Reinicke, Carmen. 2024. *Apple's $110 Billion Stock Buyback Plan Is Largest in US History.* 2 May. Accessed July 24, 2024. https://www.bloomberg.com/news/articles/2024-05-02/apple-s-110-billion-stock-buyback-plan-is-largest-in-us-history?embedded-checkout=true.

Samsung Electronics Co., Ltd. 2024. *Form 10-Q.* Suwon: Samsung Electronics Co., Ltd.

Weygandt, Jerry J, Paul D Kimmel, and Jill E Mitchell. 2020. *Financial and Managerial Accounting.* Hoboken: Wiley.

NOTES

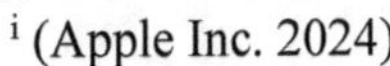

[i] (Apple Inc. 2024)

[ii] Ibid.

[iii] Ibid.

[iv] Ibid.

[v] Ibid.

[vi] Ibid.

[vii] Ibid.

[viii] Ibid.

[ix] Ibid.

[x] Ibid.

[xi] (Reinicke 2024)

[xii] Ibid.